Dream Kitchens

Dream Kitchens
The Heart of the Home

THE ART INSTITUTE OF CHARLOTTE
LIBRARY

John & Cassidy Olson

4880 Lower Valley Road, Atglen, PA 19310 USA

Pre-title page: Julie Holzman Interiors, Westport, CT
Half-title page: Peter Cadoux Architects, Westport, CT
Title page: Needham Duncan Architects, Madison, CT

Library of Congress Cataloging-in-Publication Data

Olson, John.
Dream kitchens : the heart of the home / John and Cassidy Olson.
p. cm.
ISBN 0-7643-1757-1
1. Kitchens. 2. Interior decoration. I. Olson, Cassidy. II. Title.
NK2117.K5 O57 2003
747.7'97--dc21
2002014196

Designed by Bonnie M. Hensley
Cover design by Bruce M. Waters
Type set in Zurich XCn BT/ZapfChan Bd BT

ISBN: 0-7643-1757-1
Printed in China

Published by Schiffer Publishing Ltd.
4880 Lower Valley Road
Atglen, PA 19310
Phone: (610) 593-1777; Fax: (610) 593-2002
E-mail: Schifferbk@aol.com
Please visit our web site catalog at www.schifferbooks.com
We are always looking for people to write books on new and related subjects. If you have an idea for
a book please contact us at the above address.

This book may be purchased from the publisher.
Include $3.95 for shipping.
Please try your bookstore first.
You may write for a free catalog.

In Europe, Schiffer books are distributed by
Bushwood Books
6 Marksbury Ave.
Kew Gardens
Surrey TW9 4JF England
Phone: 44 (0) 20 8392-8585; Fax: 44 (0) 20 8392-9876
E-mail: Bushwd@aol.com
Free postage in the U.K., Europe; air mail at cost.

Dedication

F.O.D. – Louie, Cocoa, and Dante!

Architects' Guild, Bethel, CT

The Kitchen Company, North Haven, CT

Contents

Opposite page: The Kitchen Factor, East Haven, CT
Right: A Matter of Style Kitchen and Bath, Cheshire, CT

The Kitchen Company, North Haven, CT

Architects' Guild, Bethel, CT

Complete Construction, Rocky Hill, CT

Acknowledgements

So many people made this book happen! We were lucky to have fabulous friends and clients who got as excited about this project as we did. The list is long but worthy of stating. Our wonderful clients who really made this happen: Kim and Simon Johnson, Ray Armstrong, Jim Ilewicz, Michael Picard, Dan Valente, Rich Finnegan, Anthony Totilo, Fran Albis, Peter and Debi Eckert, Robin Zingone, Peter Cadoux, Linda Southworth, Robbin Ricci (and Martha, Karen, and Tracy), Siobhan Daggett-Terenzi, Jan Lewis, Becky Reynolds, Gail Bolling, Kevin Kling, Trish Mauro, Lynne Persan, Tim and Susan Geitz, Peter Genovese, Mark Aldieri, Lee Vonglahn, Tony Terry, Frank Mairano, Sharon Cameron Lawn, David Duncan, Bonnie Battiston, Kerry Sheridan, and Joe Cugno. Our special friends who spurred us on: Marcia Krekoska and Jennifer Russo who said they wanted ten autographed copies, our "attorney Bernie" Vinny Cervoni, Mark Catania who thinks photography is just the coolest, Chris and Meredith Coppola who understand that each career change has moved us closer to our ultimate goal, Andrew Hull and Sue Braden who always tell us we are great; Debbie and Keith Scott and Teri and Clayton Mountain who watch the dogs while we are out late shooting, Warren and Jean Minkler who are always home for our UPS packages, Ed and Albert Lombardi who are our business mentors, Skip and Rose Fiorelli who have become personal mentors; TR Brysh for being "Steady," Lauralyn Gibson, Rob and Ruth Yost, our last connection to corporate: David Swift, Anthony and Aline Grandazzo and Jennie Allen who jumped for joy when we finished, "meter for the high-lights and let the rest fall into place" John McKeith, Nancy Ottino, and our "accountant Ernie" Steph Brodeur. Lastly, we would like to thank Tina Skinner for making this all possible.

Opposite page: The Kitchen Factor, East Haven, CT

Introduction

The kitchen. Indeed, it has officially become the heart of the home. It is the place where everyone wants to be, the source of the action! If there is any doubt where people love to be, just throw a party. Have plenty of seating in the formal living room. Make sure the entire house is spotless. Then watch! From the first arrivals to the latecomers, everyone will find their way to the kitchen.

Kitchens are people magnets. We heard it time and again while writing this book. Everything gets done in the kitchen – by every member of the family. The mail is sorted, the homework done, the tiny tots are bathed, the animals are cared for, the computer is stationed, major and minor decisions are made, and, of course, there is the preparation and clean-up of all the daily meals. It is no wonder that by the time we are adults, we flock to the kitchen at home and at parties!

Dream Kitchens was a rather accidental title. We stumbled upon it as we photographed more and more kitchens for the book. We felt that it was the perfect title for the book because every kitchen in this book was someone's dream. Every homeowner had a great story about how a particular something was desperately wanted, and a wonderful kitchen designer delivered the goods. Every single homeowner beamed with pride while we were photographing. Everyone wanted prints of the photos even though they lived in the kitchen day in and day out. On the flip side, every person who heard that we were doing a kitchen design book wanted it *that* day for ideas for a new kitchen down the road!

We quickly learned that there are two types of homeowners – those who had a new kitchen and those who wished they had a new kitchen. The push for a new kitchen is driven by the fact that the existing kitchen does not work. Nothing makes a cook crankier than a kitchen that does not work! That is where *Dream Kitchens* comes in. We have hundreds of photos full of ideas to help steer you in the right direction or at least get you thinking about what would make your kitchen work for you. The resource guide is full of people whose sole purpose in life is to assist you in making a change to your kitchen.

Siobhan Daggett-Terenzi (The Kitchen Factor, Connecticut), feels that her job is to establish a working relationship with the client that allows for glimpses into everyday life. When asked about her philosophy, she replied, "I truly believe it is every designer's responsibility to listen closely to his or her client's wishes and to share in their enthusiasm from design and selection to installation to make the entire process a memorable experience."

So peruse the book and study the pictures. See what you like and what does not appeal to you. Talk to people about their kitchens. Gather other books and magazines for even more ideas. Jot down ideas and some sketches. Then contact a kitchen designer and begin the transformation. It is our next move!

Chapter One
Glazed Kitchens

Glazing of cabinets is often a three- or four-step process resulting in a unique and dramatic outcome. The finish is usually in the one-of-a-kind category giving you a truly special kitchen. The difference between paint and glaze is obvious. Paint covers uniformly and completely. A glaze is usually painted on and then rubbed off to reveal the grain of the wood or a hint of the paint underneath. Glazed cabinets typically have more glaze around the edges and corners of the doors and cabinets giving an old, antique look. A new or old cabinet can be glazed so you have an option: replace the kitchen entirely or apply a glaze to existing cabinets for an entirely new look.

Design: A Matter of Style Kitchen and Bath, Cheshire, CT

The island features a warming drawer and ample storage. There's room for two for a quick breakfast.

Just beyond the island are a full-size refrigerator and full-size freezer.

Two sinks are placed throughout the kitchen – one in front of the window and one in the island.

The island features ample seating for family and friends.

Design: EHL Kitchens, Glastonbury, CT

The island shows off the granite counters. Cubbyholes beyond the kitchen hold coats for family and guests.

A bar is tucked into the far end of the kitchen for easy entertainment.

A desk area and a dry buffet are beyond the island.

Design: A Matter of Style Kitchen and Bath, Cheshire, CT

Bead board and a raised-leaf motif add architectural interest to the island.

A full view of the
kitchen shows the
refrigerator at one
end and the double
wall ovens at the
other end.

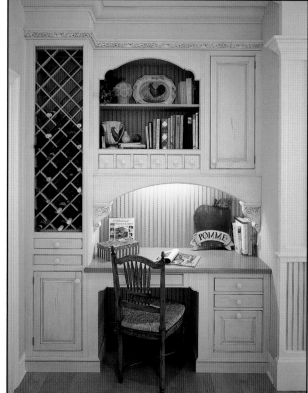

A desk at the end of the
kitchen has the same
bead board and raised
leaf detail to tie it
together with the
kitchen.

Carved moldings
and corbels create an
old world ambience.

Top: The tiered island keeps the crowds at bay while the chef prepares the meal.
Bottom: The classic work triangle is in play with the stovetop in the island and the sink across from it, the dishwasher and refrigerator not far away.

Another sink is in the island and the stovetop is opposite the double wall ovens. A pantry and desk area are just beyond in the hallway.

The cook can relax by the fire in the cozy family room while the cookies are baking!

Both the sink and the dishwasher are in the island.

Design: Needham Duncan Architects, Madison, CT; Interior Design: Bonnie Battiston Interiors, Stonington, CT; Cabinetmaker: Timothy Conti Cabinetmakers, Stonington, CT

Structural columns do double duty by supporting the ceiling and adding visual interest.

Design: American Development Corporation, Mahopac, NY

Opposite page: The double doors next to the double ovens are the cleverly disguised freezer and refrigerator.

Below: A wall length china cabinet in the kitchen is everyone's dream.

Top right: The built-in espresso maker makes breakfast taste better!

Bottom right: Granite sinks are beautiful and not very common.

A built-in hutch shows off wonderful collectibles.

Stepped upper cabinets break up an otherwise long wall.

The island with its two sinks allow two to prepare dinner.

Two dishwashers make cleanup after even the largest of parties a breeze.

Exposed beams and moldings make this functional kitchen elegant.

The large island features the sink. A bar fits perfectly into the niche created by two walls.

The desk beyond the island lets the chef conduct business without being far from the action.

Design: The Kitchen Factor, East Haven, CT

The back of the bar with its ample storage space delineates the dining area from the kitchen.

The bar area has a wine cooler, sink and microwave and extends the kitchen.

Opposite page: An piece of cherry countertop added to the back of this U-shaped kitchen creates an eating area.

Design: Homeowner; Cabinetry: Northeast Cabinet Design, Newtown, CT

Blue and white combine in this stunning kitchen.

The island has an open corner for pots.

Bookcases hold cookbooks for easy access during cooking.

Beautiful built-ins look like furniture.

Wood floors compliment the bright cabinets.

Double ovens are near the cooktop. The television and microwave are nestled in the corner near the wine rack.

A refrigerator/freezer combination is beyond the tiered island.

Design: Kling Bros. Builders, Norwalk, CT; Decorative Finishes: Faux Designs and Artistic Services by Eugenia Monte, Naugatuck, CT

Columns and an arch frame this fabulous glazed kitchen.

The details on the corners of the island gives it a furniture-like quality.

An informal dining area is off the kitchen and features built-in cabinets.

Open and airy is the name of the game in this spacious kitchen.

The ceiling detail is the cleverly disguised vent system for the cooktop.

Design: The Kitchen Company, North Haven, CT;
Architect: Anthony Terry Architects, Branford, CT

The L-shaped island keeps the party at bay while
the chef prepares the next course.

The pull knobs on the drawers and doors are a brushed metallic and square.

The wall beyond the island is home to an extensive CD collection.

Design: Northeast Cabinet Design, Newtown, CT

The neutrals in this kitchen make a bold statement.

The corners of the island and the desk are differing sizes of the same detail.

The crown molding is accentuated by the detail on the cabinetry.

Chapter Two
White Kitchens

Simple, clean, elegant, classic, bright – white fills the bill on all accounts. White cabinets allow for colorful walls and accessories. The darkest kitchen instantly brightens when redone in white. White always looks neat and clean and provides a great backdrop. Just think of the possibilities such a neutral cabinet color gives you! Colorful and fun hardware stand out against the white (we've even seen fruit and vegetable cabinet knobs and drawer pulls). Floor and backsplash tiles may be dark or colorful. Dark countertops also provide striking contrast in the white kitchen. There is truly no end to the options that white cabinets give you in the overall design and decorating of your dream kitchen.

Design: Mauro and Company Kitchen and Bath, Milford, CT; Contractor: A&M Development, Branford, CT

The island features the cooktop on one level and the eating area on another inviting conversation while cooking. The backsplash is tile with *bas-relief* adding visual interest.

Shelves on the end of the island offer storage for cookbooks and knickknacks. The side cabinet is a dry buffet and is designed to hold food destined for the adjacent dining room.

The blue tile in the backsplash and the blue window treatments carry the blue from the hood into the rest of the kitchen.

Design: The Kitchen Factor, East Haven, CT

**Old wooden floors and beams give this new
kitchen a well worn feel. Note how the
refrigerator looks like a large cabinet.**

The prep area of the island is stepped down from the sitting area and includes a small sink. Two coordinating tiles make the backsplash above the stove.

The warming drawer in the island keeps the meal warm until ready to serve. The farm sink can easily accommodate a fast clean up.

Design: *A Matter of Style Kitchen and Bath, Cheshire, CT*

The cooktop on the island allows the chef plenty of room for preparation and a view into the dining room.

Dual ovens and the refrigerator
are nestled in the corner.

The trim above the sink adds interest and connects the cabinet to the ceiling and the rest of the kitchen.

A small side cabinet doubles as a dry
buffet for large dinner parties.

Design: Northeast Cabinet Design, Newtown, CT

The granite counter extends on one end to create an eating area for three.

Left: The sink cabinet has a furniture-like appearance with the sculpted legs.

Right: The stainless steel appliances set off the white cabinetry.

A small cabinet above the refrigerator adds more
storage in a very open kitchen.

The sideboard is actually a built-in cabinet complete with under-
cabinet task lighting.

The refrigerator, the stovetop, and the double ovens line the back wall of the kitchen to keep the chef focused.

Design: The Kitchen Company, North Haven, CT; Mark Aldieri Architects, East Hampton, CT

Right: **The upper and lower cabinets frame the opening to a space beyond while providing the chef with conversation opportunities.**

Below: **The island has shelves on both ends and in the center for keeping cookbooks handy.**

Opposite page;
Top: **A second small sink is nestled into a small niche in a wall of cabinetry.**

Bottom: **The sitting/eating area also has bookshelves for storage.**

Design: Peter Cadoux Architects, Westport, CT

The wine rack surrounds the refrigerator.

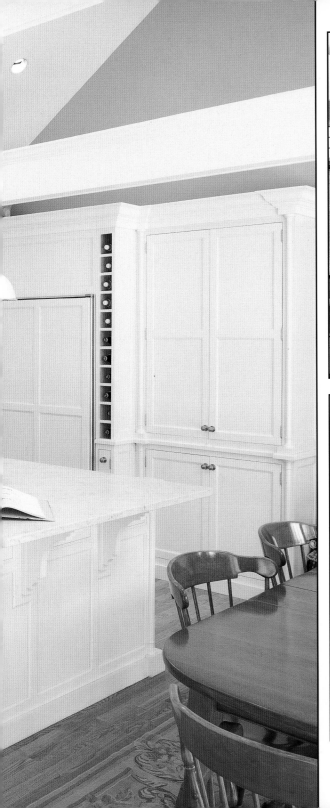

The roller blind above the warming drawer in the island hides appliances while not in use.

The turned molding on the cabinets and the ceiling beams create architectural interest in this open kitchen.

Lots of drawers are available for storage, and an interesting hood above the stovetop crowns this kitchen.

The crown molding steps to break up the wall of cabinets. The countertop is a beautiful cherry wood finished perfectly!

The stepped peninsula marks the end of the kitchen and the start to the family room beyond.

An interesting crown molding combines the upper cabinets while "decorating" the window.

The desk area and bookshelf match the kitchen cabinets and separate the kitchen from the rest of the home.

The refrigerator is paneled to match the rest of the cabinets.
The freezer drawer slides out from below the refrigerator.

Design: Needham Duncan Architects, Madison, CT;
Contractor: Regan Home Improvement, Waterford, CT;
Cabinetmaker: General Woodcraft, New London, CT

Blue and white reign in this seaside kitchen. Refrigerator and stove are next to each other.

Sink and dishwasher pair up opposite the refrigerator and stove.

Wavy glass in the upper cabinets add to the seashore theme.

White countertops and white cabinetry make this galley kitchen look larger.

The television is mounted under the counter to save the counter for cooking tasks.

Top right: The matching tile in this corner niche ties it in with the rest of the kitchen.

Bottom right: The floor-to-ceiling mirror gives the illusion that the kitchen is larger than it is.

Chapter Three
Wood Kitchens

Bird's eye maple, tiger maple, natural cherry, and quarter-sawn oak are just a few choices for wood cabinetry. Enter into the world of translucent and opaque stain and you get even greater choice. Perhaps it is the reflection of the natural beauty of Mother Nature that makes the wood kitchen so magnificent. Whether it is the rustic look of knotty pine, the traditional and bold grain of oak, or the subtle but rich grain of cherry, the wood kitchen is an excellent choice for most homes. Wood finish cabinets can and should be considered fine pieces of furniture that provide practical uses in today's kitchen.

Design: The Kitchen Company, North Haven, CT

Left: Cherry cabinets and a wall of windows were a must when renovating this kitchen to keep with the 1930s period of the home.

Center: The mosaic tile floor and the stainless appliances add to the retro feel of this completely modern kitchen.

Right: The butcher block is maple. The bead board is cherry.

Tall windows and deep sills allow for a kitchen greenhouse of herbs.

The cabinets are custom-made inset with
a bead detail on the doors.

The dishwasher is black in keeping with the marble countertops.

Lots of angles make this large kitchen inviting and interesting.

Double ovens, the microwave and the warming drawer are on the same wall.

The desk area is to one side of the kitchen to keep business rolling while dinner is cooking.

Bead-board cabinet doors add to the ambience.

The island is three dimensional!

Opposite page: The wonderful French country kitchen is a feast for the eyes.

The large island has a center triangle topped
with a coordinating granite.

The crown molding adds height. Note the detail on the corner of the island.

The refrigerator and freezer are paneled to match the rest of the kitchen.

Design: Northeast Cabinet Design, Newtown, CT

The refrigerator and dry buffet combine the kitchen with a cozy sitting area with fireplace.

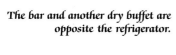

The bar and another dry buffet are opposite the refrigerator.

The cabinets follow the
curve of the bay
window.

Design: Anthony Totilo Architects, Darien, CT

Large windows take the place of upper cabinets and fill the kitchen with light.

The bench seat under the window does double duty – storage and extra seating.

A butcher block niche next to the paneled refrigerator makes preparing vegetables a snap.

Design: Albis-Turlington Architects, New Haven, CT

This cherry kitchen was designed to keep with the original style of the house – a 1930s Sears catalog home.

The stainless appliances provide all the modern amenities while looking retro.

The microwave and espresso maker are built-in.

The bar area is complete with a sink.

The refrigerator is paneled but features stainless
handles to keep with the stainless appliances.

The island has the dishwasher and the sink. Note the carved leg detail on the corner of the island.

The desk, set to one side, keeps everyone on schedule.

Seating on two sides of the island allows
everyone to sample the eats.

The refrigerator is in the center of the wall of cabinets. Note the "rivers" running through the granite.

The kitchen flows into the dining area and the sun porch.

83

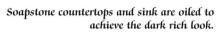

Soapstone countertops and sink are oiled to
achieve the dark rich look.

The stainless appliances and the cherry cabinets combine beautifully.

The wide-plank wood floors contrast with the cherry cabinetry.

The cooktop is on an angle and near the sink.

The glass drawers change with the season.

The backsplash above the range is
functional and decorative.

The handles on the drawers differ from the door handles.

The floor is cork for comfort on the feet.

A peninsula is near the oven and has plenty of room for a seat.

Plenty of lower cabinets provide ample storage space.

The counter steps down and in for the angled sink.

91

Design: Kitchens by Armstrong, Mystic, CT

Windows take the place of upper cabinets to keep the kitchen flooded with light.

Even the refrigerator looks like cabinetry with the paneling.

Tall cabinets are tucked next to the refrigerator.

Design: Peter Cadoux Architects, Westport, CT;
Contractor: Kling Bros. Builders, Norwalk, CT

**Stainless steel appliances compliment
the wood floors and the cabinetry.**

The granite island seats four.

The island is stepped down for the sink. Floor-to-ceiling cabinets give added storage.

Chapter Four
Modern and Contemporary Kitchens

Form follows function. As such, modern and contemporary kitchens are perhaps the most misunderstood kitchen designs. Contemporary and modern kitchens offer clean lines and stark contrasts. Modern is not necessarily contemporary but the two often marry. An Arts and Crafts kitchen can have a contemporary flair, and an Art Deco kitchen often gets a contemporary twist. Contemporary kitchens take on a life of their own with artsy accessories. Some modern kitchens have a commercial feel. Modern or contemporary – either can fit into your lifestyle, your budget, and your kitchen!

Design: The Kitchen Company, North Haven, CT

The peninsula island offers seating for two as well as a cooktop to invite conversation with the chef.

A close-up of the front of the island shows its great views of the outdoors and the fireplace.

The oversized window floods the kitchen with light even on the darkest of days. The white cabinets contribute to the open and light look and feel.

The refrigerator, dual ovens, and cooktop create an efficient working triangle.

Design: Architects' Guild, Bethel, CT

Stainless steel appliances complete the clean
look of the white cabinets.

A view of the kitchen from the sink in the butlers pantry.

Instead of an island with cabinetry, this kitchen features two wooden farm tables, one for the adults and one for the youngsters in the group.

Design: Robin Zingone Design, Chester, CT;
Cabinetmaker: AV Design, LLC, Clinton, CT

Custom-made maple cabinets complete the sleek look of this contemporary kitchen. The refrigerator peeks through from the back wall of cabinets.

The stainless steel refrigerator anchors the wall of cabinets.

The island features two ovens on either side of the cooktop. The vent for the cooktop rises at the touch of a button.

The bar, with a mirrored backsplash, is coupled with the kitchen but also stands alone.

Design: *Architects' Guild, Bethel, CT*

Upper cabinets sport glass doors and shelves to allow light into the windowless kitchen. The upper and lower cabinets form a peninsula to complete the wall of built-in cabinets down the hallway.

The niche next to the Sub-Zero refrigerator provides a spot to prepare drinks without being in the chef's way.

The warming drawer is conveniently located below the built-in oven. The built-in wine rack keeps bottles safely stored and within easy reach.

Design: The Kitchen Factor, East Haven, CT

**The granite counters are from a
fossilized riverbed, and the cabinet
handles are stick figures!**

The granite countertop and the tiled backsplash compliment each other and offset the white cabinetry.

The ovens and the refrigerator are separated by tall, thin cabinets.

The cabinets under the cooktop offer plenty of storage for pots and pans.

A cork floor adds comfort and warmth for the feet. Glass stainless steel cabinets create visual interest and compliment the stainless appliances.

The refrigerator stands off to the side within easy reach from the glasses.

The sink is under a window to afford a view while preparing or cleaning up and has a dishwasher on each side.

The granite counters compliment the white cabinets.

Each island has a cooking station; the small one has the cooktop, and the large L-shaped one has the microwave.

Opposite page: The refrigerator, the cooktop and the ovens create a triangle with the island offering plenty of space to work. The kitchen actually has two islands.

109

The opening above the cooktop allows for conversation and light to flow between the kitchen and the study beyond.

The island features the sink, the dishwasher and a place to sit to review recipes.

The study beyond the kitchen includes a place for informal meals. Note the shutters on the windows, which slide for privacy.

Design: The Kitchen Company, North Haven, CT

The beams give away the historic element of this kitchen.

The black granite counters and the white cabinets combine beautifully with the yellow walls.

The kitchen takes on a
galley-like appearance
between the cooktop
and the refrigerator.

The island is added storage space with all its drawers.

The appliance garage is sandwiched
between the microwave and the oven.

White cabinets and windows keep this kitchen feeling light.

Design: Architects' Guild, Bethel, CT; Cabinetmaker: Gregory Woodworks, Bethel, CT

The stainless refrigerator mirrors the cabinets clean lines.

The kitchen flows into the seating/eating area.

The stainless steel drawers are dishwashers.

The stainless refrigerator fits neatly next to a wall of built-ins while the tile above it ties it in with the rest of the kitchen.

Translucent glass in the doors above the dishwasher add whimsy.

This brand new kitchen looks vintage with its lighting and tile work.

The cabinetry looks more like furniture than a kitchen!

The far right cabinet opens in a "now-you-see-it-now-you-don't" fashion to reveal the ovens. A relay switch turns off the power to the ovens when the doors are closed to prevent a fire.

Chapter Five
Combination Style Kitchens

Combination style kitchens are a feast for the eyes because they combine two distinct design elements. Perhaps the island is painted black while the rest of the cabinetry is cherry. Or contrasting marble or granite is used. Perhaps two distinct styles come together in one kitchen to create a dramatic effect.

Design: Bonnie Battiston Interiors, Stonington, CT; Cabinetmaker: Kitchens and Bath Designs by Betsy House, Stonington, CT

The refrigerator has panels which match the rest of the cabinet doors to camouflage its size.

The white countertops contrast and compliment the red cabinets.

The table-for-two is actually a continuation of the cabinetry and the countertop.

123

The microwave and the oven are near each other to keep all hot foods together.

The island contains the sink and the dishwasher and continues the two-toned theme with two different granite counters.

Opposite page: The wood island and the painted cabinets set each other off. The complimentary wall colors continue the trend.

An overall view shows the painted
and wood cabinets.

The varying heights of the island create two distinct work spaces.

The sink in the island is for preparing food while the sink under the windows is larger to accommodate clean-up.

Design: Kling Bros. Builders, Norwalk, CT; Decorative Finishes: Faux Designs and Artistic Services by Eugenia Monte, Naugatuck, CT

The wall opposite the island boasts storage behind solid and glass doors.

The ovens are tucked into a corner near the dishwasher. The backsplash is on a diagonal.

Opposite page: The island is wood cabinets with a light colored marble top while the cabinets are distressed glaze and crowned with a dark granite counter.

A box soffitt separates the kitchen from the rest of the house. A small island peeks out from behind a large island that wraps around the kitchen. The large island has bead board and glass cabinets.

The small island boasts wood bead board with a wood counter and a prep sink.

All the cooking appliances – ovens, microwave and cooktop – are in line with each other for ease.

A close-up of a very functional work triangle: the sink in the island, the cooktop and the ovens.

131

Varying heights in the island countertop create two very
distinct spaces: one for work and one for sitting and relaxing.

The wall behind the island features a niche for
display and floor-to-ceiling storage.

Opposite page: Even the backsplash is in complimentary colors in this multi-finish kitchen.

Black paint on the island is the ultimate compliment to the white cabinetry. The backsplash is slate set on the diagonal for interest.

All appliances are on the perimeter while the island serves as additional counter space and storage.

The refrigerator is paneled to complete the look. The island looks like a piece of furniture with its sculpted legs.

The counter and cabinet are bumped out to accommodate the sink.

A table takes the place of an island in this wood and paint kitchen.

A warming drawer is conveniently located near an opening that looks to the dining room beyond. The upper cabinets open in both the dining room and the kitchen.

Top center: A niche next to the refrigerator boasts a sink for easy drink preparation.

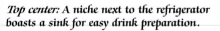

The view from the dining room: the counter is hinged to allow for food to be passed between the two rooms and the glass cabinets are two-sided to access the crystal from either room.

The dishwasher and the refrigerator are disguised behind matching wood panels for beauty and a finished look.

Design: Kling Bros. Builders, Norwalk, CT

Right: Large white columns contrast the painted island.

Opposite page;
Top: A warming drawer is below the dual ovens. Drawers flank the range for storage. A full size refrigerator completes the wall.

Bottom: A second sink and dishwasher are off to the side of the island to assist with preparation and clean-up.

The stepped island has the sink and the dishwasher as well as lots of storage space.

Design: American Development Corporation, Mahopac, NY

Pale yellow cabinets complement the cherry countertop on the island where a second smaller sink resides.

Glass doors on the upper cabinets create an open and airy look.

Cabinet doors are painted with chalkboard paint and pull out for storage. The glass doors above the drawers complete the look of the built-in china cabinet.

Design: American Development Corporation, Mahopac, NY

The island has three different heights to add visual interest and features a small circular hole cut into the granite. Use the granite as your cutting board and sweep the scraps directly into the garbage below.

The island has the sink and two drawer-style dishwashers. The green cabinet beyond the island was built as an office for the lady of the house.

Those aren't two refrigerators! One is a full size freezer.

The island holds the microwave and an ice maker on the end. The refrigerator is completely concealed to look like furniture instead of an appliance!

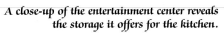
A close-up of the entertainment center reveals the storage it offers for the kitchen.

Opposite page: Soft yellow paint is complemented by deep cherry trim pieces. The entertainment center is incorporated in this pool house kitchen.

Design: Northeast Cabinet Design, Newtown, CT

The hood above the range is a dramatic detail. The backsplash is made from one solid piece of granite.

The green cabinets offer enormous storage for kitchen essentials.

Upper cabinets on the island allow sound and light to pass through in this 1930s influenced kitchen.

Another view of the island shows the breakfast area off to the side.

The column adds interest and mirrors the paneling on the refrigerator.

The plate rack allows light through to the backsplash. The faucet adds charm and interest to the sink.

The plate rack above the sink and the lattice cabinet doors add to the cottage charm of this kitchen.

Design: Joe Cugno Architects, Wilton, CT

The granite on the island is honed while the granite on the countertops are a high gloss.

The island looks like furniture with its turned legs.

A dry erase board is on the perimeter of the kitchen for quick access of phone numbers and schedules.

Built-in cubbyholes keep coats and shoes organized.

Opposite page: The perimeter cabinets are glazed while the island is painted black.

The desk area is on one end of the kitchen.

The tiled backsplash continues around the entire kitchen.

Chapter Six
Range Hoods and Backsplashes

Range hoods: some are enormous while others are discreet. Some blend into the cabinetry while others contrast it. Some are above the island while some anchor the wall with sheer size. The hood is unique to each kitchen in its finish and its placement. Backsplashes are as unique as the range hood, some are tile and others are stainless steel. Some are just above the cooktop while others continue around the entire room. Your creativity and imagination, and a little help from a kitchen designer, will guarantee that your range hood and backsplash make a statement that is uniquely you.

The range becomes almost a room in itself within the kitchen when it is surrounded by walls and tile. The lemon tree motif in the backsplash creates interest.

The tile backsplash becomes the focal point of this range. A mantle on the hood is a great place to display favorite dishes.

The hood is freestanding and stainless steel coordinating with the refrigerator.

Both the backsplash and the moldings on the hood add architectural interest.

Windows surround the hood instead of upper cabinets.

Cherry panels set the range in its own niche.

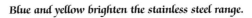

Blue and yellow brighten the stainless steel range.

Cherry and multicolored tiles create contrast between the cabinetry and the hood area.

A simple design of cherry paneling camouflages the hood.

Design: A Matter of Style Kitchen and Bath, Cheshire, CT;
Interior Design: Glenn Saltzer Interiors, Chesire, CT

Design: Homeowner; Cabinetry: Northeast Cabinet Design, Newtown, CT

Functional shelves on either side of the hood uptake add decorative storage.

Tile on the hood and the backsplash crown the Aga range.

The decorative tiles liven up the stainless hood and cooktop.

A wide shelf provides ample space for adornment.

Cabinets on either side of the range keep spices and flavorings close.

A water spout for large pots makes drawing water a breeze.

Geometric design makes this hood interesting!   **A small hood tops the glass stovetop.**

Design: A Matter of Style Kitchen and Bath, Cheshire, CT

Design: Joe Cugno Architects, Wilton, CT

Corbels and moldings make the hood spectacular.

A small niche in the backsplash is a convenient spot for spices.

Open shelves on one side and a plate rack on the other set the range and hood off beautifully.

The backsplash above the counters is tile while the backsplash above the range is stainless.

Cabinetry placed above the hood makes the most out of small places.

The stainless hood and the geometric design of the backsplash compliment each other perfectly.

The kitchen is open and airy so a bulky hood was replaced by one that rises at the push of a button on the cooktop.

The curved alcove above the range completely disguises the hood.

The stainless steel hood blends in beautifully with the cherry cabinets.

A bold backsplash makes as much of a statement as the side-by-side ovens.

Design: Northeast Cabinet Design, Newtown, CT

Design: Northeast Cabinet Design, Newtown, CT

Design: Northeast Cabinet Design, Newtown, CT; GDC, Danbury, CT

A wood hood completes the wall of cabinets.

The ceiling molding is brought closer to the cook on the hood.

The unit above the range does double duty as the vent and the microwave.

Design: Northeast Cabinet Design, Newtown, CT; Sir Development LLC, Westport, CT

Functional, elegant, . . . perfect!

Design: The Kitchen Company, North Haven, CT

A stainless steel backsplash with a shelf provides a resting spot under heat lamps until everyone is ready to eat.

Design: Lombardi Building and Design, Old Saybrook, CT

The microwave and vent system live together in this small, functional kitchen.

Design: The Kitchen Company, North Haven, CT

Tile and marble create a unique backsplash for this spectacular hood.

Design: Kling Bros. Builders, Norwalk, CT; Peter Cadoux Architects, Westport, CT

The hood contrasts perfectly with the cherry cabinets and the wall color.

Design: Mauro and Company Kitchen and Bath, Milford, CT

Tile on the hood creates a bold statement.

The tile above the range includes everything needed for a wonderful meal.

Design: Kling Bros. Builders, Norwalk, CT; Decorative Finishes: Faux Designs and Artistic Services by Eugenia Monte, Naugatuck, CT

A fruit motif continues throughout the kitchen with a medley above the double ovens.

Design: Mauro and Company Kitchen and Bath, Milford, CT

A airy kitchen with lots of windows can forgo the hood altogether.

Design: Mauro and Company Kitchen and Bath, Milford, CT

A black hood completes the look!

Design: Peter Cadoux Architects, Westport, CT

The cooktop and hood compliment the variable tile.

Design: Mauro and Company Kitchen and Bath, Milford, CT

The backsplash is a mirror to increase the size of the kitchen.

Design: Four Square Builders, Sandy Hook, CT

Appliqués on the hood dress it up!

The tile continues above the hood for a interesting design element.

Sleek and clean is the name of the game for this range hood.

The cooktop is in the island so a hood rises from the counter at the touch of a button.

The distress timbers and the stucco make this hood all Tuscany.

Chapter Seven

The Butler's Pantry

The modern day butler's pantry takes on a multitude of tasks and comes in a endless variety of shapes and sizes. The butler's pantry houses serving dishes, china, crystal, silverware, party utensils, alcoholic beverages, mixers, and more. It goes by butlery, butler's pantry, bar, caterer's kitchen and dry buffet. It traditionally is a separate room off the kitchen. However, as kitchens become more of the heart of the home, some butler's pantries are off to one side or end of the kitchen. Precious few in America have butlers, but the love affair with the butler's pantry affects everyone. Perhaps it is the connection to the past, or a more decadent time, that invokes the craving for a tiny niche of space. Perhaps it is the wide array of names that convinces us that we need it. Or perhaps it is the extra space that can become whatever we need it to become at the drop of a hat that has us forcing kitchen designers and architects to create one. Wherever you want your butler's pantry, and by whatever name you call it, do enjoy!

Design: Mairano and Associates, Canton, CT

The butler's pantry is also the caterer's kitchen.

Design: A Matter of Style Kitchen and
Bath, Cheshire, CT, Glenn Saltzer
Interiors, Chesire, CT

An extra refrigerator and microwave
complete the pantry.

Design: Kling Bros. Builders, Norwalk, CT

Design: The Kitchen Factor, East Haven, CT

The pantry is just off the dining room to make setting the table a breeze.

This open pantry can also double as the bar during large parties.

A sink and dishwasher, in addition to the ones in the kitchen, make cleanup a breeze.

Glass doors on one side let inventory be taken in a flash. A second refrigerator/freezer combination comes in handy for large parties.

177

Beautiful granite completes the storage area.

The wine cooler, refrigerated doors and ice maker are in a perfect line for a quick drink.

Design: Mairano and Associates, Canton, CT

Upper cabinets with glass doors make a beautiful and functional place to showcase fine crystal.

This pantry includes a warming drawer.

Design: Mairano and Associates, Canton, CT

Design: The Kitchen Factor, East Haven, CT

The window lets light in while allowing the butler to view who is arriving.

The counter is cherry set off by the patina sink.

This butler's pantry houses the washer and dryer and the "now-you-see-it, now-you-don't" ironing board.

The ironing board makes an appearance.

A farm sink and cherry counters combine perfectly.

A copper sink and interesting tile coordinate with the granite.

ch country pantry has lots of cubbyholes.

Bead board backsplash and hammered copper in the sink take on simple elegance.

The countertop and the bead board are cherry.

The cherry counters continue on the other side of the pantry.

Design: Needham Duncan Architects, Madison, CT; Interior Design: Bonnie Battiston Interiors, Stonington, CT; Cabinetmaker: Timothy Conti Cabinetmakers, Stonington, CT; Contractor: Point Company Builders, East Lyme, CT

Design: Mauro and Company Kitchen and Bath, Milford, CT; A&M Development, Branford, CT

Soapstone counters complete this large pantry.

One side is for the bar and the other side is for dishes.

A desk was added "for the butler".

A full service kitchen is the butler's fate in this whimsical pantry.

Design: Peter Cadoux Architects, Westport, CT

Design: Anthony Terry Architects, Branford, CT

The wine cooler connects both sides of this L-shaped pantry.

The counter contrasts wonderfully with the white cabinetry and the yellow walls.

Design: The Kitchen Design Group, Monroe, CT

Design: Sharon Cameron Lawn Interiors, Providence, RI

The backsplash is varying sizes of tile.

The butlery becomes the potting shed!

A small bar is squeezed to one side in this cherry butler's pantry.

The blue tile provides color and interest.

Design: Mauro and Company, Milford, CT

The ice maker is on one end and the wine cooler is on the other.

An extra dishwasher for the drink glasses helps when the party is over.

The dry buffet features plenty of storage.

The butler's pantry goes public . . . as the bar!

About the Authors

John and Cassidy Olson are renowned professional interior and architectural photographers with years of experience recording some of the finest homes throughout the country. A husband and wife team, they specialize in photographing interior spaces, exterior structures, and designed landscapes. Together, they bring extensive photographic experience and creativity to each assignment. They reside in Connecticut with three dogs. Their detailed images help you see first hand just how beautiful a dream kitchen can be!